A Celebration of Wiltshire in Poetry

AMANDA HAMPSON

Illustrated by
SHEILA HALEY

THE HOBNOB PRESS

First published in the United Kingdom in 2019

by The Hobnob Press,
8 Lock Warehouse, Severn Road, Gloucester GL1 2GA
www.hobnobpress.co.uk

British Library Cataloguing in Publication Data
A catalogue record for this book is available from the British Library

ISBN   978-1-906978-71-6 (paperback)
           978-1-906978-72-3 (casebound)

Typeset in Adobe Garamond Pro 12/14 pt.
Typesetting and origination by John Chandler

For Mum and Dad

Contents

Introductory Note

In the summer of 2016, on a perfect afternoon with blue skies and a light breeze, I sat down on our garden seat on the lawn, and penned a poem inspired by our lovely Wiltshire garden. This was my first visit to the world of poetry since childhood, and I knew instinctively that I had found a wonderful and fulfilling pursuit for retirement. This book, *A Celebration of Wiltshire in Poetry*, is the culmination of a year's work inspired by the natural history, landscape and heritage of this beautiful county. Wiltshire has a distinctive and ancient natural landscape, which is perhaps overlooked by travellers who pass through it, in search of coastal destinations further west. Hopefully I have captured some of the character of the county, in the diverse, and perhaps random, subjects that follow, and as such, this has been a wonderful journey of exploration, and expression of self.

This book would not have been possible without the unwavering support of three people, to whom I give my grateful thanks: first I wish to thank Sheila Haley, my friend and neighbour, who produced the beautiful and detailed illustrations to accompany my poems, and with whom I had a most enjoyable artistic collaboration; my husband Keith, for his patient assistance, valuable comments and steadfast support throughout; finally I thank John Chandler of Hobnob Press, for all his help in ensuring a smooth publication process, and for taking a chance on a novice poet.

I hope you will enjoy reading this collection of illustrated poems.

Amanda Hampson
March 2019

Great Expectations

As he rode across the Vale of Pewsey in the early 1800s, the old political crusader William Cobbett described the landscape that was the foundation for his 'land of promise, or great expectation': the combination of downland, hillside and meadow, which are basic to the Vale's agricultural history. The expansive downland in Wiltshire is notable for its huge sweeping fields, and this uniqueness prompted the poem *Land of Promise* in the set that follows.

Much of Wiltshire consists of wide open spaces, with sparse woodland, and slumbering hills that are utterly black after nightfall – take a look at the hills north of the road from Pewsey to Devizes, which are traversed by the White Horse Trail, equally brooding and atmospheric by night or day. But many of the Wiltshire hills, Woodborough and Knapp for instance, are crowned by distinctive clumps of trees, which to the observer appear to stand guard over the land below them – hence the opening poem – *Sentinel*.

Continuing the theme of inky blackness, the vast Wiltshire skies can be a source of fascination for the amateur astronomer; perhaps the absence of many large industrialized towns contributes to night-time clarity for stargazing. My last poem in this group is very short, but says everything I want to about the *Wiltshire Night Sky*.

It seems that from whichever angle you look at the wonderful *Martinsell* Hill, the dark lone pine is visible, and this was my inspiration for the poem of the same name – this lonely tree sweeping its branches over all below it.

Characteristic of the Wiltshire chalk downland are the *Eight White Horses*, featured in the fun poem at the end of this section. For the energetic walker, these carvings are best seen on the 90-mile White Horse Trail. A ninth white horse, sometimes included with the Wiltshire group, is carved on the Berkshire Downs at Uffington in Oxfordshire.

Sentinel

Valleys scored by ancient droves,
brooding hills crowned with thickets and groves.
The wintry lattice clawing a pinking sky,
rooks circling nests with a plaintive cry.

These ancient glades, sentinels of pasture,
guardians of downland, a natural arbour.
Their windward shoulders, denuded and bent,
clinging to landscape of feudal descent.

The wind gathers her cloak and bustles through,
the Vale bursts with life and the chalkhill blue.
The lichened copse sets out her green stall,
burgeoning trees flutter in a leafy shawl.

Meadows sway with buttercup and daisy,
larks ascending to a blueness made hazy.
Rivulets run clear, laughing under bridges,
hare and badger gouge the ditches.

The spinney in its fullness, keeper of the Vale,
a haven for wildlife under its veil.
The canopy mosaics against the starburst sun,
farmers amble home when the day is done.

Martinsell

Climb the furrows to one-tree hill
and see to the ends of mists, yet still

from a thousand feet, and with stooping boughs,
I see farms below with sheep and cows.

My seat a fort atop The White Horse trail,
moated by copse and chalk of the Vale.

Bend with me to the Giant's mound,
Fiddlecase and Hassocks on flinty ground.

Lean on the wind to Starling's Roost,
over to Wansdyke and rails in disuse.

My softwood branches bow to the floor,
where the canal meanders and buzzards fly o'er.

Sweeping away to Rainscombe and Oare,
follow the contours and hear the wind roar!

Climb the furrows to one-tree hill,
where the boughs of a pine are lonely still.

Land of Promise

Hillsides *fruitful of grasse and corn,*[1]
edged with skirts of *oak, ash and thorn.*[2]
This Vale of farms, fertile and sturdy,
especially good for whete and barley.[1]
Sheep-worn downland grazed and scuffed,
coarse with bents and grassy tufts.
A Turfe rich and fragrant with thyme and burnet,[3]
a vision from Aubrey we'll not forget.
Lowland meadow an artist's dream
of dabs and swirls of purple and green,
on shimmering yellow and cornflower blue,
with swards of red and sheep's fescue.
Round-headed rampion, orchid and thistle,
rich pasture for centuries the home of cattle.
This Vale of Pewsey,
this chalkland history,
this vision of Cobbett's
Land of Promise.

[1] Anon traveller circa 1540.
[2] William Shakespeare, A Midsummer Night's Dream.
[3] John Aubrey.

Wiltshire Night Sky

Clouds blushed by the setting sun
are time-lapse chased away
on autumn winds.
And a soundless indigo mantle
falls, pinned to the universe
by a thousand twinklings
light-years away.

Eight White Horses

Across Pewsey Vale
and o'er the Downs,
on a 90-mile trail
through villages and towns,
eight famous carvings the rambler will find,
White Horses of Wiltshire, they're ancient signs.

In mangers of grass
lie the figures of chalk,
eyes made of glass,
some trot, some walk.

On Bratton Down, the oldest,
the original with crescent tail,
and with long legs, the biggest,
emblazoned on the Vale.

Devizes' horse is the latest to the stable,
it's seen from far away,
in the Millennium, according to the fable,
'twas lit up until New Year's Day.

The carving on Cherhill Down,
it strikes a walking pose,
four miles east of Calne,
close to where the Kennet flows.

Broad Town horse has a view
from the far end of the Vale,
almost lost after World War II,
this symbol of strength prevails.

Close to the ancient Ridgeway track,
Hackpen horse has a trotting pose,
the head was once built up with chalk,
'til rain washed away all but the nose!

Marlborough horse on Granham Hill
is the smallest of the eight,
College groundsmen care for it still,
and now it's walking straight.

Pewsey horse is one of the newest,
best seen from the track below,
an earlier one was overgrown and lost,
'til erosion allowed the head to show.

From the canal bridge at Honeystreet,
see the horse at Alton Barnes,
where Walker's Hill and Milk Hill meet,
'twas paid for twice, so say the yarns.

Across Pewsey Vale
and o'er the Downs,
on a 90-mile trail
through villages and towns,
On Wiltshire's most famous walk,
eight White Horses carved in chalk.

Something about Trees

Trees are wonderful things – they are the lungs of the world, and a most efficient food-producing system. They feature strongly in this next group of poems, which also take much of their inspiration from the year-round richness and variety of nature reserves in Wiltshire. The Wiltshire Wildlife Trust now manages at least 38 reserves around the county, encompassing meadows, chalk downland, wetlands and woodland, and ranging from one hectare of disused railway at *Hat Gate*, to sweeping downs and lakes further south.

It is hard to believe that the *Big Belly Oak* in Savernake Forest is around 1100 years old; 'what other living thing saw Harold defeated, Jane Seymour courted?' But this ancient tree still stands, together with other similarly aged oaks – it is thought that nowhere else in Europe is there such a concentration of veteran trees.

There is a wonderful sensuality to be experienced upon entering the darkness of a *Beech Wood* after light rain – smooth bark the colour of mink, and glistening lime-coloured leaves – and to my mind beech trees produce the best colours in autumn – rich golds and russets. The beeches of West Woods are, for me, as much an attraction as the carpets of bluebells beneath them in May.

And walking between the houses near the fire station in Ramsbury, across a leat, and emerging in the magical Ramsbury Meadow, was certainly a throwback to childhood and fantasies of a *Secret Garden!*

Big Belly Oak

Big-bellied and squat
sit I, with cankered knots,
gnarled and carbuncled,
old limbs peduncled.
Callused fingers,
commensal creepers,
a tumoured bole,
a rotten hole.
A lumbering old man
With arthritic knuckles
and ugly notches.

But mine is a story
of ancient glory.
What other living thing
saw Harold defeated,
Jane Seymour courted?
And beneath
my lichen waistcoat
the sapwood is rising,
heartwood softening.
Big-bellied and squat
Sit I.

Bluebells of West Woods

Early in May
a carpet of near-violet
rolls out,
creeping between trees
and smothering footpaths.
And this woodland world
is filled with
the scent and colour of bluebells.
Come inhale the spring!

And when the rain comes,
the opening canopy glistens with lime,
beech bark smooths to otter brown,
and recurved flower tips
tremble with every drop.

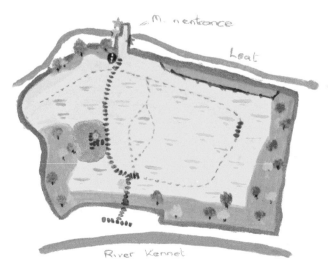

KEY

——— Reserve boundary	···· Footpath
Woodland	IIIIII Boardwalk
Wet woodland	✦ Gate
Marshy	✦ Vehicular gate
Pond	✦ Stile

🛈 Information board	
● Seat	
III Steps	
⊢•—• Fence	

Within the map:
- M. nentrance
- Leat
- River Kennet

Secret Garden

If I was a child,
it would be so exciting,
to push through the hedge
at the end of the garden,
unhook the old wooden gate,
and cross the leat
to the secret garden
at Ramsbury Meadow!

Skip along the boardwalk,
over trickling streams of mud and chalk.
Safe from the bog and silty ditches,
stroke hairy comfrey and tufty sedges.
See boatmen and skaters, a pond duet,
catching butterflies with an old blue net.
Wonder aloud at the emperor dragonfly,
chase all about the blue-tailed damselfly.
Count golden marigolds and yellow iris,
listen out for the springtime songstress.
Dangle legs from the dipping platform,
even from there smell the stinky hawthorn.
Watch the ripples from moorhen and coot,
a swan glides into view, snapping at my boot.
Twist and turn with swift and swallow,
hide under the curtains of weeping willow.
If I was a child at Ramsbury Meadow!

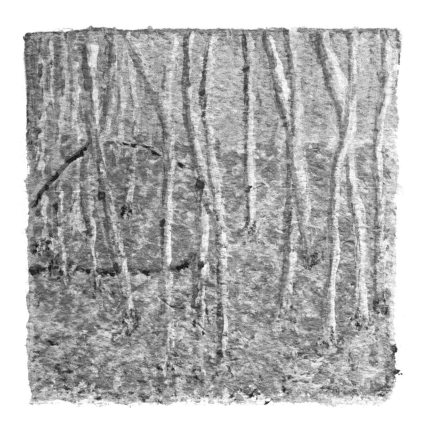

Beech Wood

Thirty years ago or more,
from the rustling forest floor,
a verdancy stirred.

From a whispering shade,
a murmuring glade,
sapling beeches awoke.

A canopied kingdom,
gold in autumn,
an umbriferous wold,

a bower to behold.
The handsomest of trees,
bending in the breeze.

Hat Gate

In the quiet of early January
under cloud-locked skies,
when nothing seems alive
and nothing has light,
we stumbled upon a place
to stir the senses of
the unguarded explorer.

Where once the old railway
snaked its way boldly
through Savernake,
the old earthbanks
are now a wildness
of untrammeled growth.

Tangled maybush and bramble
choked with Traveller's Joy,
with its silvery tufts
like fibres on a cotton boll,
or wisps of hair
on a happy old man.

Shining vermillion rose-hips
painting the tips
of woody skeletons,
and lush and vivid moss,
a cloying opportunist
on fallen logs.

And our nostrils flared
at the fermenting carpet

of crab apples,
crushed and wasted
on the floor
of this railway graveyard.

Brick and Stone

Though my poetry in this book is perhaps less inspired by buildings and architecture, than by the natural landscape, I found a few notable exceptions on my roamings.

Two churches in particular caught my imagination, for very different reasons. A cycling trip to Marden revealed some unexpected treasures – one of which was the stained glass in All Saints' Church. The casual visitor is invited into the church by warm southerly sunlight streaming through the window in the wall of the chancel. The glass in the south chancel is one of only two sets of stained glass at All Saints', and unusually depicts a vivid composite of the Wiltshire landscape; inspiration indeed! It was designed by Molly Kettlewell and installed in 1979.

St Matthew's Church at Rushall stands mysteriously apart from the village. A little bit of research revealed that in the 1800s, the Lord of the Manor cleared local dwellings away from the vicinity of the church, enabling it to dominate its lovely pastoral setting; in fact a small mound near the graveyard conceals the remains of the manor itself!

At 123 metres, the cathedral spire in Salisbury is the tallest in England, and it can indeed be seen from far away. Such an elegant piece of architecture, beautifully captured by Constable in his painting of 1831, a tranquil scene that has changed little over time.

The elegant *Rainscombe House* nestles in a punchbowl softened by dense deciduous trees that are glorious in autumn, always encouraging the motorist to glance sideways when passing through Oare on the A345.

The final poem in this group – *Six Avebury Stones* – is somewhat of a departure: my first effort at the sestina, a poetic form dating from the 12th century, and using so-called lexical repetition – can you work out the structure?

The Spire

Look up and gasp, at the 400 foot spire,
by artists and authors it's truly admired.
Seen from all around, it draws the eye,
punctures the clouds, high in the sky.
Taller than Norwich and Coventry too,
Chichester and Lichfield next in the queue.
It guards the Chapter House with the Magna Carta,
the best kept copy of the people's charter.
Without buttress and arch it would have fallen,
like Malmesbury Abbey and Lincoln, for certain,
but Christopher Wren came to the rescue,
his beams and pillars a definite breakthrough.
Constable's view has changed little over time,
his pastoral depiction is still sublime.
Glorious nave, transepts and choir,
beautifully finished by the magnificent spire.

Rushall Church

I am cast back in time
by the sight of this little church,
encircled by sheep-trodden turf,
and dew-sodden pasture
stretching to the edge of vision.
The flinty wall of a haha
suffocates with sphagnum,
its time-worn hollows
probed by small brown birds.
And in the sepia distance,
shafts of evening sunlight
sweep the dappled landscape
of farm, byre and copse.
The graveyard
weighs heavy
with tilted tombstones
stifled by lichens.
And buried nearby,
the old remains
of a vanished manor,
whose owner created
this splendid isolation.

The Thatched Cottage

Swallows swoop to the sheaves,
rodents wriggle through,
bees buzz under the eaves,
the brick has a Wiltshire hue.

Thatch skirts the windows,
like a fringe in your eyes,
see the ribbons of chasing sparrows,
smoke coiling into the skies.

Hornbeam guards the gate,
swinging on its hinges,
a well-trodden path of slate
leads up to old rose arches.

There's a smile on the door,
peeling paint and a battered knob,
straw on the kitchen floor,
a large pot on the hob.

A cosy glow from the snug,
a cat stares out from the sill,
flowers spill from a jug,
the curtains have a chintzy frill.

On the roof a straw hare boxes
against the low blood moon,
clematis trails the fences,
it will soon be June.

Rainscombe House

Oft when climbing the road through Oare,
I'd glance through etiolated trees,
towards a grand stone-washed house
looking south through lightless windows.
Set centre stage in an amphitheatre
of contours studded with perfect trees,
like florets of cruciferous vegetables,
or mushroom clouds
from perfect explosions.

Marden Church

'I will lift up mine eyes unto the hills, from whence cometh my help'
Psalm 121

Warm southerly sunlight
streams through kaleidoscopic glass
in the window of the chancel.

Look closer
at the spectral mosaic

Of lumbering cyan hills
meeting inky skies,
bleeding to smalt, azure.

Of sweeping flaxen farmland,
xanthic, ochred,
aureate, gilded.

Of verdant meadow and pasture,
viridescent
with the greenness of beryl.

Of rolling opaline downland,
a chalky White Horse,
and Monet haystacks.

An iridescent composite,
a chromatic tribute to
The Vale of Pewsey.

Six Avebury Stones

Guarding henge gate is the Blacksmith's Stone
Sixth in the arc stands the Barber's megalith
Keeper of the southern gateway is the Devil's Chair
A fluted stone marks the site of the mighty Obelisk
Two large stones stand together as The Cove
Looking for its lost partner at midnight is the Diamond

Balanced on one of its corners is the Diamond
Felled in medieval times was the Blacksmith's Stone
Shadows of the solstice are cast by stones of The Cove
Legend has it the barber was crushed under the megalith
At the centre of a sarsen circle stood the Obelisk
Near to the road sits the Devil's Chair

A natural seat in the stone explains 'the Devil's Chair'
Standing for 4500 years is the Diamond
Probably the tallest stone at Avebury was the Obelisk
Stukeley tells us the blacksmith removed the fallen stone
Keiller uncovered the barber's skeleton under the megalith
Fertility rituals were practised at The Cove

The largest megalith at Avebury is seen at The Cove
The seat has long been a resting place at the Devil's Chair
The barber's medieval scissors were found under this
    megalith
Legend says that spinning through 360 degrees is the
    Diamond
Keiller rebuilt the remains of the Blacksmith's Stone
Towering above other Avebury stones was the Obelisk

Thought to have been a phallic symbol, the Obelisk
One of the first features of Avebury was The Cove

The megalith was returned to the arc as the Blacksmith's
    Stone
It is said the Devil can be summoned at the Devil's Chair
Also known as the Swindon Stone is the Diamond
The barber lay for 600 years in a grave under his megalith

And now it is known as the Barber's megalith
Flanked by much smaller stones was the Obelisk
At the northwest quadrant you come face to face with the
    Diamond
Two stones are standing, and two have fallen, at The Cove
Many pagan legends surround the Devil's Chair
An iron wedge is still buried near the Blacksmith's Stone

The mighty Obelisk was probably the tallest, The Cove the
    largest
Alive with legend are the Blacksmith's Stone, Barber's
    megalith and the Devil's Chair
And still the Diamond looks for its lost partner at midnight

Four Seasons

Seasonal changes, and all that they bring to the natural world, are a rich source of inspiration to the writer with an affinity for the countryside. The five poems that follow all have elements reflecting the four seasons, and were a joy to compose.

Spring and autumn are my two favourite seasons, and *Spring at Marden* and *Ripening at Southcott* are two of my favourite poems in this collection. I can feel the pale spring sunshine on my face every time I think of the cycling trip to Marden; the setting was so evocative of Van Gogh's Almond Blossoms. And catching the low October sun shining through the orchard on the road out through Southcott, literally stops you in your tracks.

How beautifully Sheila Haley captures the essence of a flower meadow in summer, in her illustration of *Meadow at Jones' Mill*, which is indeed a very special place. And even though we sat on Wilcot Green in autumn, 'chestnut leaves cracking under our feet', we had a strong sense of the Green in summer, with its village fete. The latter poem is written in the form of a Shakespearean sonnet, in which the final rhyming couplet is a defining feature.

Residents of Burbage and the surrounding area will know that the village has a large and well attended annual Christmas tree sale in the churchyard. My choir is usually invited to sing at this event, and I recall one year being vaguely amused by us being positioned outdoors in the only shaded spot, on a sunny but utterly freezing December day! Hence the light-hearted mood of *Christmas at Burbage*, which is also written in the form of a sonnet.

Spring at Marden

A pale spring day took us to Marden,
bicycles whirring past a flint-walled garden.

Blossoms trembling against sun-washed blue,
dainty on twisting almond as Van Gogh drew.

Gazing upwards into the giddying haze,
drunk on his inspiration on that most tranquil of days.

Bathed in the astonishing beauty and gaiety
he had observed in his search for serenity.

Imagine his brush strokes of impressionism,
the brilliance of colour in his divisionism.

The decoration and patterning in Japanese art
touched his work and captured his heart.

Hope and awakening at Saint-Remy,
still life, the subject of his Japonaiserie.

A pale spring day took us to Marden,
to see the almond tree in the flint-walled garden.

Village Green at Wilcot

Sitting on a bench, on the Green at Wilcot,
horse chestnut leaves cracking under our feet,
we couldn't have found a nicer spot
for an autumn picnic, it's such a treat.
Pub at one end, canal at the other,
clematis-clad cottages in between,
there's a cricket club further over,
idyllic really, for a village green.
A perfect pitch for summer fetes past,
craft stalls and cakes in candy-striped tents,
pet shows and donkey rides, kids having a blast,
and villagers smiling on, from over the fence.
Packing up the rucksack in the fading light,
wandering home, inspired to write.

Ripening at Southcott

One day in early autumn,
on an oft-trod path
south through leafy lanes,
my walker's step
was arrested
by the sight of the orchard;
a golden kaleidoscope
in shafts of October sun.

Plumping, sweetening fruit
blushing, shining, smiling,
soft thudding to an earthy bed.
Nutbrown bruised
and fermenting
in the dampening mould.
Sharp effervescence
on the ripening air.

A glut from bended tree
with its
autumn-ochred leaves
in silent senescent fall.
A dwindling canopy
of yellowing mosaic
against a pale
and fading light.

Christmas at Burbage

In the shade of the churchyard yews
are stacked Christmas trees a-plenty,
prospective buyers jostling in queues,
hoping one will take their fancy.
The Nordic non-drop are very pleasing,
bushy and tall, perfect for the hall,
pretty with frost on this wintry morning,
baubles available from a nearby stall.
Beryl Cook characters chattering and browsing
seasonal crafts with berries and holly;
under the gazebo the choir is gathering
for a rendition of God Rest you Merry
Gentlemen of the village looking festive as Santa,
sleighs pulled by reindeer with twigs for antlers.

Meadow at Jones' Mill

I

I took the path to the little meadow,
my first tread
long since the frigid dormancy of winter.
That I might find delight
in the whispering grasses
and swaying oxeye.
How tall the bents and sedges
and Yorkshire Fog!
Sprung dry from the
clodded earth,
parched from the
late summer sun.
Wading through thirsty stems
I found a spot
to sink to the cool ground
and nestle in the wildness;
watch the sun bleed over the hill
and squint at the big sky,
a purity of clouds and blue.

II

Ethereal seed heads of the dandelion clock,
ground hugging leaves of plantain and dock.
Cranesbill and cornflower,
campions and clover,
a colour palette for the wild flower lover!

Blue blue flax calms the fiery poppy,
buttercup and daisy, fragile beauty.
Flowering grasses,
water-loving sedges,
delicate seeds catch summer breezes.

Foxtail and horsetail brush the wanderer,
thistle and teasel spurn the admirer.
Elegant the willowherb,
meadowsweet always superb,
sheltering the lark's nest – do not disturb!

A Bit of Fun

There is no doubt that reading the work of poets, both those of renown and those less well known, and an awareness of the poetry community generally, allows the writer to develop his/her craft. The poems that follow in the next section have perhaps been influenced by the style of greats such as John Betjeman and Pam Ayres, if I may be so bold as to suggest a connection.

In his delightful anthology of Six Poets, Hardy to Larkin, Alan Bennett tells us Betjeman may be pretending he writes 'light' verse when in fact it isn't; he may not write poetry of ideas or argument, but because it is simple doesn't mean there's nothing to understand. Though I can't say for certain that all of Betjeman's and Ayres' poetry is rhyming, I have yet to find a piece from either of them that does not; they have both achieved great success from this literary tool. Like Betjeman, Ayres is an accomplished and most entertaining performer as well as a poet, as I discovered at her session at the Cheltenham Literary Festival in 2018.

Seven out of the nine poems that follow are rhyming. To pen such poetry is great fun, as long as is doesn't become too contrived for the sake of finding words that fit! Pewsey and Marlborough feature in this set of eight, as well as the famous A303; I seem to think the latter is the subject of at least one book title? I have also squeezed in a limerick, about a fictitious *Pewsey Woman*. A five-line limerick is written using a particular rhythmic pattern: the first two lines and the final line are rhyming, and the third and fourth lines rhyme. I hope you will find some fun on the next few pages!

The Moonrakers

This is a story of brandy and cheese!
Of customs men who were easily conned,
when smugglers, keen to avoid being seized,
hid their contraband in a nearby pond!
The Swindon wool boys had a favourite tipple,
but brandy and gin came with a very high levy.
The barrels slipped into the pond, not a ripple,
raked out after dark by the smugglers with glee.
When caught in the act by the customs men,
they said they were raking a rather large cheese!
'Twas actually the reflection of the moon in the fen!
And amused by this simple-minded tease,
the customs men laughed and went on their way,
and so the legend lives on today.

Marlborough Town

I was married in Marlborough Town,
swept down the street in a slub silk gown.
From St Mary's at one end
to St Peter's at t'other,
I gaily wandered to meet my lover.

I was married in Marlborough Town,
near the College of world renown.
From graveyard cedar
to the Green Dragon Boozer,
I trailed over cobbles to happy ever after.

I was married in Marlborough Town,
a lily bouquet and a daisy crown.
Family and friends
at the Castle and Ball,
gathered around at the great Town Hall.

I was married in Marlborough Town,
up to the Common for a right-royal hoe-down.
From Kingsbury Terrace
to the elegant Green,
a joyous couple, picture the scene!

The Canal at Pewsey

R eeds and rushes half drinking, half drowning,
in moveless waters.
Loosestrife proud against angry nettles
colour-spiked with willowherb,
cow parsley straining to see,
scabious nodding below.

Moorhens drift towards sunless banks,
voles slip soundlessly
into unseeable depths.
Wren perches up above,
throttled in song,
and the heron lifts up into majestic flight.

Beside the muddied towpath,
cracked dry from rainless skies,
barges huddle like lumbering beasts
jostling at a waterhole.
Cargos of wheelbarrows, logs and geraniums,
thin smoke coiling from tin chimneys.

Pewsey Station

Clickety-clack, clickety-clack,
trains come thundering down the track.
Travellers hurry along the road,
heads down in commuter mode.
Briefcase in one hand, phone in the other,
conversation is way too much bother.
Stop for coffee at the 'Italian Job',
steaming cappuccino only a few bob!
Into the waiting room out of the cold,
green leather chairs and photos of old.
Last few passengers over the bridge,
fashionably late for the first class carriage.
Great Western Railway mainline to Penzance,
perhaps there's time for a little romance?
Clickety-clack, clickety clack,
trains come thundering down the track.

Seaside or countryside?

Slimy seaweed and empty shells
Silty sand and sucking sea
Spiny sea urchins and stinging jellyfish
Squawking gulls snatching food
Barnacled boats and battered beach huts
Driftwood, detritus and dirty deckchairs
Lilos and limpets, crabs and crustaceans
Flotsam and jetsam and flying frisbees
Kiss-me-quick hats and candy floss
Oh I don't like to be beside the seaside!

But how I love the countryside!

Wild meadows with larks ascending
Shady banks with primrose and campion
Busy hedgerows with birds a-chatter
Sweeping views to distant hills
Woodland havens of beech and birch
Streams tumbling over otter-brown stones
Patchwork fields of happy wheat
Grassy farm tracks and lines of poplar
A glade, a copse, an arbour, a heath;
this green and pleasant land.

A303

The County crossover is soon after Andover
Wave to Jensen Button, as we pass by Thruxton
On to Amesbury, not far from Salisbury
Just round the bend, we crawl past Stonehenge
Skirting the Plain, is it faster than the train?
Wave to Wylye Down, across fields of mainly brown
And the Valley of Wardour, many an arbour
Suddenly at Cranborne Chase, it feels like a race
Halfway is Mere, Stourhead is near
Dropping a gear, let's pull in for a beer
Ah – services at Wincanton – a pit stop on the marathon
Then speed past Castle Cary, and I think an old dairy
Bypass Yeovil to the Blackdown Hills
It's like a switchback the 303 – thrills and spills!

Pewsey Woman

There was a young woman from Pewsey,
most everyone thought her a floosie.
When she went to the pub,
all the men called her scrub,
it's a pity she wasn't more choosey.

The River at Marlborough

Shoppers rushing hither and thither,
oblivious of the nearby river.
Mallards preening,
dippers dipping,
kingfishers fishing,
willows weeping,
daffodils dancing,
pondweed straining,
swans nesting,
herons wading,
fishes leaping,
voles hiding.
Shoppers rushing hither and thither,
oblivious of the nearby river.

The Old High Street

I live in the old butcher's shop,
so say the local history books.
Hanging baskets out the front,
under the eaves on the old butcher's hooks.

This must have been the post office,
pillar box and phone booth standing guard.
The PO counter is now a kitchen counter,
but you can still post a card!

Imagine the rosy-cheeked baker
with a tray of buns, a dozen,
out in the street to cool,
straight from the oven.

The old picture house stood here,
today a paper shop and bookmakers.
Guess TV killed trips to the flicks,
and what happened to the drapers?

Look up! At the grand bay windows.
A bustling department store no more,
out-of-town retail parks
killed it off for sure.

The old chapel is on the village green.
Peer in through the arched window,
now a sitting room with pews and a font,
the ones in the old sepia photo!

The schoolhouse playground
is now a parking lot full of cars.

The old classroom bulging with boozers,
the newest of the village bars!

And on the corner the Phoenix Hotel,
once the scene of a few bashes.
Turned into swanky apartments,
seems to have risen from the ashes.

Birds and Bees

I had never seen snowdrops in such great numbers, until I moved to Wiltshire. But since hearing of the Shepton Mallet annual Snowdrop Festival in neighbouring Somerset, I have wondered if the huge clumps and carpets of snowdrops we see in February every year have anything to do with the origins of this festival. The story goes that James Allen (1830–1906) was the first person ever to breed new varieties of snowdrop from the wild plant, and he lived in Shepton Mallet. Allen grew all the species and varieties then known, and was probably the first person to cross them deliberately and raise hybrids from seed. This final set of poems, including *Snowdrop*, was inspired by our natural history, mainly flowers and birds, and, as mentioned in the *Introductory Note*, some of them were penned in the setting of our Wiltshire garden.

Poets can write about the smallest of things or ideas, and I very much enjoyed writing about single flowers – the snowdrop, peony and wisteria. And as a lover of birds since childhood, they feature in four of these poems. The idea of tiny birds like the wren, belting out the loudest song in springtime, and of our dear robin befriending the gardener, were a rich vein for inspiration! And the magnificent red kite, now commonly seen over Wiltshire, soars the skies majestically 'with barely a wing-beat'.

This book has been a joy to compile, and I hope you have enjoyed reading this poetry of Wiltshire as much as I enjoyed writing it.

Herald the Spring

Atop the tallest tree,
the thrush as lord sings he.
Plum-breasted amid the blossom,
the chaffinch trills his anthem.
The goldfinch flits and twitters,
a merry note that never alters.
The dunnock hops this way and that,
his muted song a little chat.
And the great tit with its many calls,
are they just to deceive us all?
The collared dove flies from its cot,
and our robin, nesting in a pot,
pairing up for mating,
they are not for waiting.
Ah, the wren, the loudest of them all,
despite him being so small!
But I love the blackbird the most,
perched on a chimney top he boasts
his throaty twilight call,
as darkness and dew doth fall.

A Wiltshire Garden

Warblers and wrens trilling from the hedge,
the lazy cry of the buzzard overhead.
Mint and marjoram, lavender and sedge,
roses blooming from every bed.
Brick and bark, rich textures brown,
a haven of trees, far from town.

Daisies bowing to the lawn,
sweeping grass now turning fawn.
Iris and loosestrife craning over water,
climbing pear clinging to mortar.
Burgeoning fruit plentiful on the bough,
blackcurrant and blueberry – ready now!

Birch leaves fluttering in the breeze,
jasmine reaching to the sky with ease.
Ferns peeping out from the hebe full,
moss creeping over every wall.
Bees and butterflies happily abound,
nature toiling without a sound.

Pergola

Coral-pink petalled rose,
perfume of childhood gardens.
Pricking all who go near.

Dangling lanterns of white wisteria,
May-time beauty beyond belief.
Littering the ground with ugly pods.

Delicate palest jasmine
reaching for the sky.
Strangling its woody support.

Late-flowering anemones,
dancing bottle-green foliage.
Straining under their own weight.

Clematis smiling at the sun,
lilac petals of tissue paper.
Shrivelling to brown handkerchiefs.

Damson and orange fronds of
the honeysuckle flower.
Sometimes they smell, sometimes not.

Tendril

You thought I was dead,
my old wood strangling the trellis.
But tendrils sprouted up top,
snaking, curling,
hopelessly feeling for support,
and then you cut me down.

You thought I was dead,
but I still sprouted fresh and green,
a leafless plant organ
with a life of its own,
snaking towards you,
even when you cut me down.

You thought I was dead,
still green and succulent,
still snaking and curling,
even after falling to the ground.
And you felt repulsed.
Your punishment for cutting me down.

Monarch of Winter

Proud to usher in winter,
   the rufous-breast trills forth,
a little downy throat swollen in song,
blush bosom tumescent with effort.
What impossible, tuneful notes
from a tiny upturned beak!

And this little sovereign
in songful solitude,
bold bravery allows
to befriend the tiller of the soil;
flitting, darting, hopping
to the worker's furrow.

And he,
heavy with greying brume,
boreal gloom,
clay sodden boots,
is lightened
by fleeting feathered tameness.

Then away, away
to skeletal trees.
Smudged berry redness,
rouge-chested splendour,
warbling once more
against a pinking winter sky.

Peony

Bury your face
wantonly
in her lusty pinkness.
Ice-cream petticoats
of raspberry-marbled lace.
Lift your head
from her heady redolence,
and watch the bee
penetrate
her fists of brazen blooms,
craving the drink of the gods,
and staggering from her
trembling meringued skirts.
Where the bee sucks
there suck I!
Coquettishly
she tips her head
and spurns
the butterfly
to the breeze.

Red Kite

This elegant emperor,
once absent from the skies,
now darkly glides
into urban view.
Angled wings twisting,
kite-tail swivelling,
such graceful mastery!
Soaring audacity!

Belly of chestnut,
russet fingered wings,
a feathered cloak
of dazzling white.
Beaded glassy eyes
ablaze with amber,
this rakish raptor
back in our skies.

Silently hunting with
barely a wing-beat,
then swoop and dip
and hover over prey.
A thin mewling,
wavering squealing,
fanned tail trailing
before twisting away.

Fox

High in the sky
a lunar glow,
glistening trees bowing,
heavy with snow.

Sharp frosted breath
our lungs to fill,
his vulpine shadow
shrouding the hill.

Fur thick and wild,
an urban beast,
a furtive tread
in search of a feast.

Now in solitude,
soft midnight prowl,
arboreal quietude,
flap of an owl.

Swish of brush,
loud howl cracks the night,
in marmalade clothing
he slips out of sight.

Swans at Bowood

And then, flying in to take charge,
the outstretched necks of swans,
their V-shaped skeins making an entrance.

The silvered lake stippled by the breeze,
shivering at their arrival,
bracing itself for touchdown.

The swoosh echoing around sweeping parkland
of sweet chestnut and poplar, trembling
at the majestic landing.

Sailing with a tundra-white hull,
wings slightly open, proud and guarded,
coverts cupped like water lilies.

galanthus

Snowdrop

Buried am I
beneath this tree
in wintry sod.
Huddled close
to other bulbs,
swollen and shiny
from last year's glut.

No-one sees,
no-one hears,
my vernal push
of emerald shoots
through winter's
mossed and
frosted floor.

Reaching for light
from the lengthening days,
feeling for warmth
from the hastening spring,
head hanging low
I emerge
in winter's last chill.

Collar-high
in fresh-blown snow,
my brave milk-flower
trembles,
dancing happily
with the brightness
of a new season.

About the Author

Amanda Hampson (neé Adams) was born in 1959, and lived in Leigh-on-sea in Essex before attending University College Swansea, and subsequently the University of Aston in Birmingham, to study environmental biology. After a career principally as an editor in science and medicine, spanning over three decades, Amanda retired in 2015. Her professional life included several years as an editor at the *Lancet* medical journal in the mid–1980s, and work abroad in over 20 countries. As a contrast to her working life, she is now delightfully engaged in various branches of the arts, including singing, amateur dramatics and poetry. She is also a keen walker and tennis player. She has lived in Wiltshire with her husband Keith since 2013.

The Artist

Sheila Haley has lived in the Vale of Pewsey for nearly twenty years. After retiring from a long service in schools administration, she joined a local group 'So you think you can't draw!' where she discovered her gift for painting and drawing. Sheila has found the Wiltshire countryside and her love of village life are strong inspirations for her art works, and her varied and detailed illustrations beautifully accompany the poems in this book. Sheila enjoys a very busy and active retirement – she has been involved in community projects and was a police chaplain, and she is also a keen badminton and table tennis player. In addition, Sheila enjoys spending time with her three children and grandchildren.

Lightning Source UK Ltd.
Milton Keynes UK
UKHW022251030719
345504UK00007B/46/P